DALAI
LAMA

Cath Senker

WAYLAND

First published in 2016 by Wayland
Copyright © Wayland 2016

Editor: Elizabeth Brent
Designer: Elaine Wilkinson

ISBN 978 0 7502 9768 4

Printed in Malaysia

10 9 8 7 6 5 4 3 2 1

Picture credits: Cover: (left) viplash/Shutterstock.com, (right) ddp USA/REX Shutterstock; p1: (top) sarawuth wannasathit/ Shutterstock.com, (bottom) BEN STANSALL/AFP/Getty Images; p3: Anthony Ricci/Shutterstock.com; p4: BEN STANSALL/ AFP/Getty Images; p5: Cath Senker; p6: Fine Art Images/Heritage Images/Getty Images; p7: dibrova/Shutterstock.com; p8: Popperfoto/Getty Images; p9: ullstein bild via Getty Images; p10: RAYphotographer/Shutterstock.com; p11: sarawuth wannasathit/Shutterstock.com; p12: Bettmann/CORBIS; p13: STR/AFP/Getty Images; p14: Popperfoto/Getty Images; p15: Keystone-France/Gamma-Keystone via Getty Images; p16: AFP/Getty Images; p17: arindambanerjee/Shutterstock. com; p18: Anthony Ricci/Shutterstock.com; p19: SAM YEH/AFP/Getty Images; p20: Zzvet/Shutterstock.com; p21: atiger/ Shutterstock.com; p22: Shyam Sharma/Hindustan Times via Getty Images; p23: Sameer Ashraf/Barcroft India/Barcoft Media via Getty Images; p24: SIPHIWE SIBEKO/Reuters/Corbis; p25: BEN STANSALL/AFP/Getty Images; p26: Eric VANDEVILLE/Gamma-Rapho via Getty Images; p27: Asianet-Pakistan/Shutterstock.com; p28: Purbu Zhaxi/Xinhua Press/ Corbis; p29: Lewis Tse Pui Lung/Shutterstock.com

Background images and other graphic elements courtesy of Shutterstock.com.

A cataloguing record for this title is available at the British Library.

Wayland, an imprint of Hachette Children's Group

Part of Hodder & Stoughton

Carmelite House

50 Victoria Embankment

London EC4Y 0DZ

An Hachette UK Company

www.hachette.co.uk

www.hachettechildrens.co.uk

CONTENTS

BUDDHIST LEADER

On a hot, sunny day in June 2015, several thousand people in a football stadium in southern England eagerly await the arrival of His Holiness, the Dalai Lama.

Despite the crowds, calmness reigns. There are Tibetans, from the elderly to babies, many wearing traditional colourful dress. They mingle with Western Buddhists from various traditions and others interested in the Dalai Lama's teachings on how to live a better life. A woman beams proudly: outside the stadium, His Holiness has just blessed her young son.

HIS HOLINESS ENTERS

Several groups of traditional Tibetan and Nepalese dancers entertain the crowds while they wait. Finally, the Dalai Lama enters the stadium and all stand to welcome him respectfully. Although elderly, he walks tall like a man decades younger and gives his message slowly, clearly and cheerfully, often smiling and laughing.

▶ His Holiness the Dalai Lama makes the namaste welcome gesture

► Tibetan musicians on the football pitch in traditional costumes

DEVELOPING COMPASSION

He explains that we can't buy peace of mind; it doesn't come from outside. We have to fight against emotions such as hatred, anger and jealousy. Then we can develop compassion from within and become tolerant towards others. It doesn't matter whether you're a Buddhist, a follower of another religion, or have no faith at all. Everyone can practise developing a calm and healthy mind.

BUDDHIST LEADER

But who is the Dalai Lama? Known as His Holiness in Western countries, he is the Buddhist spiritual leader of the people of Tibet, a remote, mountainous land ruled by China, to the north-east of India.

The Dalai Lama works towards a better understanding between religions and for justice for the Tibetan people. Although he is hugely popular among ordinary people worldwide, he is also a figure of controversy. World leaders sometimes refuse to meet him and some Buddhists protest against him. This book explains why, as well as describing the extraordinary tradition of Dalai Lamas, the life and ideas of the current Dalai Lama and the debate over whether the tradition will die with him.

Awards

The Dalai Lama has received more than 150 awards, including:

• 2011: Mahatma Gandhi International Award for Reconciliation and Peace

• 2010: International Freedom Conductor Award

• Honorary degrees from 45 universities worldwide

Leabharlanna Poiblí Chathair Baile Átha Cliath

Dublin City Public Libraries

5

THE DALAI LAMAS OF TIBET

There have been just 14 Dalai Lamas since the tradition began in the Middle Ages.

In the late 14th century, the belief arose in Tibet that religious leaders called Dalai Lamas could reincarnate. A Dalai Lama was a past spiritual leader who had been reborn in a new body to continue his good work in the world.

OCEAN OF WISDOM

The first Dalai Lama was Gedun Drupa (1391–1474) and the second was Gedun Gyatso. The third, Sonam Gyatso, received the title Dalai Lama from the Mongol chief Altan Khan. Khan appreciated Sonam Gyatso's great intelligence and knowledge and wanted to honour him. The title, which means 'Ocean of Wisdom', was then applied to the first two.

▶ A statue of the Third Dalai Lama, Sonam Gyatso

▶ Potala Palace
in Lhasa, Tibet

TIBET

The fifth Dalai Lama, Lobang Gyatso, was the first to become the ruler of Tibet as well as its religious leader. A great scholar, he began the building of the Potala, the winter palace of the Dalai Lamas in the Tibetan capital Lhasa, which still stands today as a museum.

During the 19th century, there were four Dalai Lamas who all died young, and both the British and the Chinese tried to seize control of Tibet. In the Chinese Revolution of 1911–12, the Tibetans pushed out the Chinese. In 1913, Tibet declared its independence under the rule of the 13th Dalai Lama (1876–1933), who gained more political power than any Dalai Lama since Lobang Gyatso. Tibet remained an independent country until 1951.

Reincarnation

Buddhists believe that when someone dies, their soul is reborn in another body, human or animal. Your fate in your next life depends on your karma – your actions – in this life. If you behave well, you will enjoy the results of your karma and be reborn as a human. If your actions are bad, you will be reborn at a lower state, as an animal. Tibetan Buddhists believe that Dalai Lamas choose the body into which their soul will be reborn.

BECOMING THE DALAI LAMA

▲ The 13th Dalai Lama,
Tubten Gyatso, in 1900

How do Tibetan Buddhists find out which baby is the reborn Dalai Lama? It's a long and complicated task.

Luckily, when the 13th Dalai Lama died in 1933, he left a clue. After his death, his face mysteriously turned towards the north-east. The high lamas (spiritual leaders) knew to travel in this direction from the capital, Lhasa. They made their way to the holy lake of Lhamoi Lhatso, hoping for further signs. Gazing upon the lake, Reting Rinpoché, the leader of the search, saw a vision of a monastery with a turquoise and gold roof. A path led from it to a small house with strangely shaped gutters.

DISCOVERY!

The high lamas searched far and wide for this house. Four years later, in 1937, they finally came across it in Taktser, north-east Tibet. Living in an ordinary farming family, they found two-year-old Lhamo Dhondrub, an unusual toddler who loved all people and animals and seemed to understand their feelings. He hated to see any suffering.

High lama Kewtsang Rinpoché had brought some of the 13th Dalai Lama's possessions to see if the child recognised them. He showed Lhamo the prayer beads. 'This is mine!' cried the child. After many more strict tests, the high lamas were convinced they had discovered the true 14th Dalai Lama, and he was given the religious name Tenzin Gyatso.

A MONK'S TRAINING

In 1940, the five-year-old Dalai Lama was brought to the Potala Palace in Lhasa to begin his training as a monk. It was hard for the little boy. He was separated from his parents and siblings and not allowed to mix with other children, except for one brother, Lobsang Samten, who lived with him until the young leader was eight.

The Dalai Lama used to glimpse the outside world from his palace through binoculars. He was supposed to study until adulthood, but events were to push him into leadership much faster than expected.

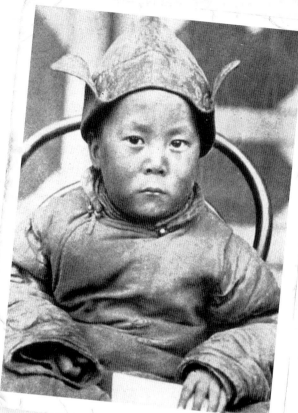

▲ The 14th Dalai Lama, aged four

The Dalai Lama's education

The Dalai Lama studied logic, Tibetan art and culture, Sanskrit, medicine, and Buddhist philosophy. He had to memorise Buddhist texts and learn the art of debating.

THE BUDDHIST FAITH

Buddhists follow the teachings of Gautama Buddha, a sage, or wise man, on whose teachings Buddhism is based.

These teachings focus on living peacefully with others, and not harming anything or anyone. Buddhists believe that people have a responsibility to care for each other, and for all living beings.

◀ A drawing of Gautama Buddha in meditation

THE FOUR NOBLE TRUTHS

The Buddha taught that there are Four Noble Truths. The first is that human beings endure suffering: poverty, disease and pain. They also suffer because they don't own all the things they want. The second is that suffering is created by our desires. It is in our minds. If we don't get what we want, we may become upset, angry or jealous of others. These negative emotions make people do bad things – cheating, stealing or even killing.

The third truth is that we can be free from suffering if we understand that it is in our minds and not real. The fourth is the Eightfold Path, which shows people how to be free from their desires.

▶ Buddhist monks in Thailand accepting offerings of food

THE EIGHTFOLD PATH

To follow the Eightfold Path, people should lead a balanced life, allowing themselves some comforts but not too many luxuries. They should try to:

1 – Accept the Buddhist teaching about suffering

2 – Be unselfish, and compassionate towards other people, understanding their point of view

3 – Tell the truth and speak in a helpful way

4 – Be kind and thoughtful in everything they do, so that they don't behave badly and regret it afterwards

5 – Choose work that is useful to society and doesn't damage the environment

6 – Live wisely and encourage good actions

7 – Be mindful of what they are thinking, feeling and doing to avoid behaving badly

8 – Meditate regularly, spending time being quiet and still to train their mind and body to be peaceful; being at peace helps people to act in a sensible way.

Ideas for all

Everyone can follow Buddhist ideas, whether or not they are Buddhists. As the Dalai Lama says,

'I am interested not in converting other people to Buddhism but in how we Buddhists can contribute to human society, according to our own ideas.'

TROUBLE IN TIBET

▲ Chinese forces build a bridge to invade Tibet, 1950, while troops are transported on rafts.

In 1949, a Communist government came to power in China. Determined to seize control of Tibet, China invaded the country in October 1950.

In normal circumstances, the young Dalai Lama would have quietly continued his education. But at this time of crisis, the people needed a leader, and so he became the ruler of Tibet, at the age of just 15.

OCCUPIED BY CHINA

Until 1950, Tibet was an isolated country, with its own culture, language and religion. Most people were farmers, and there was little economic development. There were no roads; people walked everywhere and carried goods on yaks.

However, in 1950, Tibet was made part of the People's Republic of China. This was very controversial. Most Tibetans felt that their country was being taken over by a foreign power. Yet the Chinese thought that Tibet was part of China. They believed that they were freeing it from an old-fashioned economic system that forced most people to stay in one place and do farm work for their local landowner.

▶ 1959: Tibetan monks lay down their arms after an unsuccessful uprising, surrounded by Chinese troops.

PEACEFUL PROTEST

The Dalai Lama made many peaceful attempts to stop the takeover. He asked the Chinese leaders to leave Tibet alone, and sent messengers to the USA, Britain and Nepal to ask for support. No one would help. His Holiness also tried to stop Tibetan guerrilla fighters from attacking the Chinese, believing this would only lead to loss of life on both sides.

The 1951 treaty

In 1951, a Tibetan delegation was ordered to go to the Chinese capital Beijing and sign a treaty. It allowed China to set up military and civil (non-military) headquarters in Lhasa but said that Tibetans could rule themselves. In fact, China now ruled Tibet.

However, Tibetan fighters did resist the Chinese. In 1956, there were clashes in the east of the country, which soon spread to central Tibet. In March 1959, an uprising broke out in Lhasa. The Chinese Army crushed the protests, and tortured and killed captured fighters. The Dalai Lama knew the Tibetans couldn't defeat the Chinese Army, and that he could no longer lead his people in his own country.

LIFE IN EXILE

On 17 March 1959, the Dalai Lama and his helpers disguised themselves as ordinary Tibetans and slipped out of his palace in Lhasa.

Luckily, a sandstorm blew up, forcing the Chinese soldiers to cover their faces so they didn't notice the silent group of Tibetans escaping.

TREK TO INDIA

At the edge of Lhasa, the group crossed the Kyichu River in little boats, praying that Chinese soldiers would not spot them. Then began an exhausting trek over the Himalayan Mountains to India, in freezing temperatures. The Dalai Lama became ill but mostly he worried about his people in Tibet. When the Chinese crushed the uprising, around 2,000 people were killed.

▶ The Dalai Lama (third from the right), fleeing from Tibet across the Himalayas

WELCOME IN INDIA

Two weeks later, the Dalai Lama reached India. Crowds lined the streets to greet him – many had come from miles around to receive his blessing. Indian Prime Minister Jawaharlal Nehru welcomed him, and by November, 30,000 of his fellow Tibetans had arrived as refugees.

▲ The Dalai Lama (middle) meeting with Jawaharlal Nehru (left), just after his arrival in India

GOVERNMENT IN EXILE

In June 1959, the Dalai Lama officially rejected the agreement that China had forced Tibet to sign in 1951. He set up a government in exile in Dharamsala in India and began creating a society to preserve Tibetan religion and culture. The Indian government helped by setting up schools for Tibetan children, and building monasteries.

The Dalai Lama also appealed to the United Nations (UN), which strongly disapproved of China's abuse of human rights in Tibet. However, no action resulted – no country wished to oppose China. There remain 120,000 Tibetan refugees living in India today.

Democracy

The Dalai Lama's new government in exile was democratic – Tibetan refugees worldwide elected the parliament. People were free to say or believe what they liked, to hold meetings and to travel. The Dalai Lama was even prepared to give up his own power if two out of three Tibetans voted to take it away.

ON THE WORLD STAGE

For the past half a century, the Dalai Lama has travelled to more than 67 countries in six continents, speaking to political leaders and ordinary people about Buddhism and campaigning tirelessly for justice for Tibet.

In 1967, the Dalai Lama began travelling to learn about different countries and explore ideas about how to modernise Tibet. He also hoped to help others understand Tibetan religion, culture and problems.

▲ The Dalai Lama receiving the Nobel Prize in 1989

HUMAN RIGHTS ABUSES

In 1973, His Holiness visited Europe for the first time. He spoke about human rights abuses in Tibet, where Chinese people were taking over land and resources and destroying Tibetan culture – monasteries, paintings and holy books. People admired this wise but modest leader and were shocked to hear what was happening in Tibet. They were inspired by His Holiness's message about peaceful campaigning and set up organisations to campaign for freedom for Tibet.

▶ Tibetan Canadians march for Tibetan human rights in 2010.

NOBEL PEACE PRIZE

In 1989, the Dalai Lama was awarded the Nobel Peace Prize for his non-violent campaign to end the Chinese rule of Tibet. Accepting the prize in Norway, he said,

'The awarding of this prize to me, a simple monk from faraway Tibet, fills us Tibetans with hope. It means we have not been forgotten.' He decided to give the prize money to hungry people in the world, people with leprosy in India, and a Tibetan charitable organisation founded on Buddhist ideas.

WORLDWIDE MEETINGS

In the early 21st century, His Holiness continued to travel widely. He has met several times with President Barack Obama of the USA, who calls him a 'good friend' and agrees that Tibetans should have more freedom under Chinese rule.

All are equal

The Dalai Lama dislikes formality – he sees himself as an ordinary human being and treats everyone he meets as an equal. He says laughter and smiling are unique human features and we should use them more to bring people together.

TEACHER AND WRITER

Even though he is elderly, the Dalai Lama is still an active leader of Buddhists worldwide and teaches all year round.

The Dalai Lama gives teachings in his home city of Dharamsala, which are usually free to attend. Every year, he gives his annual spring teachings for 15 days. Several thousand people, both Tibetans and non-Tibetans, gather for these popular events. His Holiness's words are translated into English and broadcast on the radio so thousands more can hear them.

▶ His Holiness in prayer during a visit to the USA

A PACKED SCHEDULE

His Holiness travels extensively to give teachings and talks to Buddhists and non-Buddhists. His schedule would be exhausting for most people half his age. In just five weeks in 2015, he gave a four-day teaching in India, a public talk in London, then another four-day teaching in India. These were followed by another talk in the USA and a celebration of his 80th birthday.

▶ The Chinese edition of *My Land and My People*, the Dalai Lama's life story

BOOKS ON BUDDHISM

The Dalai Lama communicates his ideas through his books too. He has written or co-written more than 110 titles about Buddhism, his own philosophy for how to promote human happiness, and universal ethics – how all people, whether religious or not, can lead a good life. He has also described his discussions with scientists about the links between Buddhism and science. For example, the Dalai Lama says that in both fields, knowledge must come firstly from things that are observed rather than read about.

Kalachakra Initiation

His Holiness leads the Kalachakra Initiation ceremony several times a year, both in India and abroad. It is a ceremony for student monks who have completed their training. During eight days of preparation, Buddhist monks make a sand mandala, a picture that stands for the universe. On the ninth day, the students arrive. They vow to be compassionate towards all living things and to work to help others. Once initiated, the students go out into the world as monks.

WORKING FOR A BETTER WORLD

The natural world is close to the Dalai Lama's heart, and he speaks out about the damage we are causing to wildlife and our environment.

In 2006, His Holiness was horrified to discover that tiger skins were being imported to Tibet to make chubas, traditional coats. These coats had originally been made of sheepskin. Tibet's use of the skins was contributing to the extinction (wiping out) of tigers in Asia.

TIGER-SKIN TRADE

Out of respect for their leader, many Tibetans destroyed the tiger skins, although they were worth about two years' wages. The word soon spread throughout Tibet and by 2013, Tibet's tiger-skin trade had ended.

▶ Tibetan refugees in Nepal wearing traditional sheepskin coats

▶ Roads
have been built
into the mountainside
of the Tibetan highlands.

DESTROYING THE FORESTS

His Holiness also campaigns against the destruction
of wildlife and forests in Tibet. Before Chinese rule,
animals in Tibet did not fear humans because as
Buddhists, Tibetans did not kill or harm them.
Birds roosted in the middle of busy human settlements,
and flocks of sheep and yaks grazed close to people.
But under Chinese occupation, forests were burnt
down for wood and animals hunted for food.

The destruction of forests has had a devastating impact
on other countries, too. Tibet is the source of many rivers that
run through Asia. Without trees to absorb water and keep the soil in
place, the soil has been eroded and rivers have silted up – the silt
raises the water level so when it rains heavily, the rivers flood.

In 2010, His Holiness broadened his message to express
concern about the effects of climate change on the natural
world and resources. He urged world leaders to make
addressing climate change a top priority.

Climate change

On the Tibetan
Plateau, temperatures
are rising at more
than twice the
average global rate.
If the Himalayan
icebergs melt, the
consequences for
the region could be
disastrous.

THE DALAI LAMA'S DAY

The Dalai Lama sees himself as a simple Buddhist monk and lives modestly. For him, religious practice is completely intertwined with his daily life.

His Holiness always rises extremely early and he loves the quietness at this time of the day. When he's at home in Dharamsala, he wakes up at 3 a.m. and showers. He prays and meditates until 5 a.m., and salutes the Buddha. Then he goes for a walk. If it's raining, he walks on a treadmill instead. At 5.30, he eats a simple breakfast of traditional Tibetan porridge made from tsampa (barley powder), with bread and jam and a cup of tea. He often listens to the BBC world news in English.

PRAYER AND MEDITATION

From 6 to 9 a.m. he continues his meditation and prayers, moving on to the study of Buddhist texts and philosophy. The Dalai Lama also reads the newspapers and official papers to do with his work. Lunch is at 11.30 a.m. and is always vegetarian – although when he's travelling, His Holiness eats the food he is offered, whether or not it is vegetarian.

◄ The Dalai Lama taking part in prayers at a temple in Dharamsala, India

AUDIENCES WITH THE DALAI LAMA

If he needs to discuss work or hold interviews, the Dalai Lama visits his office from 12.30 to 3.30 p.m. He usually has at least one interview along with several meetings with Tibetan and non-Tibetan visitors. Evening tea is around 5 p.m. and afterwards he sometimes watches TV. Then it's time for evening prayers and meditation, and he goes to bed around 7 p.m. The Dalai Lama's routine varies depending on his commitments, but he always sticks to his morning and evening prayers and meditation.

▶ His Holiness during one of his regular interviews

A life of prayer

As well as spending several hours in prayer and meditation every day, His Holiness also prays in spare moments during the day, when he is eating or travelling. There are prayers for every activity, from waking to eating and sleeping. For him, 'religious practice is a 24-hour occupation.'

CONTROVERSY AND CRITICISM

Not everyone shares respect for His Holiness. The Chinese government strongly opposes the Dalai Lama, accusing him of seeking to rule Tibet, and he is the number-one enemy of the Shugden Buddhist sect.

In 2011, the Dalai Lama stood down as Tibet's political leader in exile, although he remains its spiritual leader. He no longer campaigns for independence for Tibet but calls for religious and cultural freedom for Tibetans under their own regional government within China. Yet the Chinese government still sees him as a threat.

KEEPING CHINA HAPPY

World leaders sometimes refuse to meet the Dalai Lama because they don't want to upset China. China is a major economic power, and other countries need to do business with it. In 2014, the Norwegian government refused to meet His Holiness when he visited Norway, and later that year, South Africa denied him permission to attend a meeting of Nobel Peace prizewinners. The other prizewinners protested, and the meeting was cancelled.

▶ South Africans protest against their government's refusal to allow an earlier visit by the Dalai Lama in 2011.

THE SHUGDEN PROTESTERS

A group of Western Buddhists worship the god Shugden. They are from the Gelugpa sect, one of the five sects of Tibetan Buddhism. Their leader believes members should read only the scriptures of their sect and study only with their own lamas.

The Dalai Lama, who is also from the Gelugpa sect, criticised this approach, arguing that all sects should enjoy equal respect. The Shugden Buddhists turned against him. Its members call him a 'false Dalai Lama' and a 'dictator' and argue that he does not permit religious freedom. When the Dalai Lama appears in public, they protest against him. The Chinese government gives money to the Shugden sect because it also opposes the Dalai Lama. However, the Dalai Lama has no control over the Shugden Buddhists, so he couldn't possibly curb their freedom. He thinks they should study the history of Buddhism, which accepts all different sects.

'Religion should never become a source of conflict, a further factor of division within the human community.'

25

INTERFAITH DIALOGUE

The Dalai Lama promotes dialogue between people of different faiths to seek common ground and learn to work with each other.

He believes different religious traditions suit different kinds of people, but people from the various faiths can live peacefully together. To him, all religions have the same basic message of love, compassion, forgiveness and tolerance. If everyone practised their religion seriously, the world could become a compassionate community. He suggests showing compassion towards your enemies and trying to understand their point of view. This is what he has done when dealing with Chinese leaders.

DIALOGUE WITH RELIGIOUS LEADERS

His Holiness enjoys exchanging views with the leaders of worldwide religions – he has met several popes and was particularly good friends with Pope John Paul II (1920–2005). He says people of all different faiths can learn from each other. At a 2011 inter-faith meeting in Minnesota, USA, Rabbi Michael Lerner told the Dalai Lama that his faith was strengthened by the Buddhist idea of letting go of the desire for new things.

▶ The Dalai Lama meeting with Pope John Paul II in 2003

DOING GOOD IN THE WORLD

In the Dalai Lama's view, no one of faith should cause bloodshed. He believes that Islamic extremists who carry out violent attacks in the name of Islam are not true Muslims. Yet he also recognises that Western policies in the Middle East, such as the US-led invasion of Iraq in 2003, created anger and resentment that led to extremist protest movements. As an alternative, His Holiness urges religious communities to become involved in their society and respect people's rights.

▲ Muslims give more to charity than people of any other religion. These volunteers are giving out goods to needy people in Quetta, Pakistan, for the Muslim Eid festival.

WORKING TOGETHER

His Holiness also encourages cooperation between people of faith and those with none. Everyone can promote basic human values and warm-heartedness, which build trust and friendship. You don't need to be religious to have peace of mind and treat others gently.

'I look on religion as medicine. For different complaints, doctors will prescribe different remedies. Therefore, because not everyone's spiritual "illness" is the same, different spiritual medicines are required.'

THE LAST DALAI LAMA?

What will happen when the Dalai Lama dies? Will the tradition die with him?

The Chinese government has stated that the next Dalai Lama must reincarnate in China and be recognised by the Chinese government. This would allow China to choose a Tibetan leader to fit with Chinese political interests.

THE END OF THE DALAI LAMAS?

To Tibetans, the idea of dictating where the Dalai Lama will be reborn is completely wrong. In Buddhism, no one can control another's reincarnation. The Dalai Lama says that when he's 90, he will consult with the high lamas and Tibetan people about whether the Dalai Lama system should continue. If they decide it should, then it will. And if so, the next Dalai Lama might be a man – or woman – born in exile outside Tibet but not in China.

▶ A night-time view of modern Lhasa in 2015 – the Dalai Lama has never been able to return there.

HOPES FOR DEMOCRACY

His Holiness would prefer Tibet to be completely democratic, with an elected leader and equality between men and women. Society has changed greatly since the Dalai Lama system developed, so it is out of date. He believes that China needs democracy and human rights too. In the early 21st century, Chinese people protested for democracy; in Hong Kong in 2014, thousands of young protesters took to the streets. In His Holiness's opinion, the world should encourage China to become democratic and to respect Tibet's culture, language and environment. He is content to be the very last Dalai Lama if he leaves behind a fairer system of government for his country.

'When the day comes for Tibet to be governed by its own people, it will be for the people to decide as to what form of government they will have. The system of governance by the line of the Dalai Lamas may or may not be there.'

GLOSSARY

climate change Changes in the earth's weather, including temperature, wind patterns and rainfall, caused by the increase of gases in the atmosphere – especially carbon dioxide

compassion Sympathy and a desire to help others

controversial Involving disagreement or debate

democracy A system in which the people vote for their leaders

exile When a person is forced to leave their country

guerrilla A member of an armed group of soldiers who are not part of a regular army

His Holiness The term Western Buddhists use for the Dalai Lama

honorary A position given as an honour without the person having the usual qualifications for it – for example, you do not have to pass exams to receive an honorary degree

initiation Becoming a member of a group through a special ceremony

karma The sum of the good and bad actions in a person's life, which Buddhists believe will decide what happens to them in the next life

lama A title given to a spiritual leader in Tibetan Buddhism. It is believed that most lamas are reincarnations of previous spiritual leaders

logic The science of thinking about the reason for something

meditate To focus the mind on something for a period of time in order to become calm and peaceful

monastery A building where monks (members of a male religious community) live together

Mongol One of the people of Mongolia, an area now part of China

occupation When a country takes control of another country using military force

philosophy The study of the nature and meaning of the universe and human life

refugee A person forced to leave their country, usually because of war or natural disaster

reincarnate To be born again in a new body

revolution When a group of people change the government of a country, often using violence

Sanskrit An ancient Indian language used for writing Buddhist texts

sect A small group of people who belong to a particular religion but who have some beliefs or practices that separate them from the rest of the group

silt Sand or mud that is carried by flowing water

torture Causing somebody severe pain in order to punish them or make them say or do something

United Nations An organisation formed of many countries of the world that aims to solve political problems in a peaceful way

uprising When a group of people join together in order to fight against the people who are in power

vision A dream of a religious kind that brings information or ideas

Further information

Websites

http://kidworldcitizen.org/2012/02/03/learn-about-the-dalai-lama/

http://education.nationalgeographic.co.uk/media/next-dalai-lama/

Books

Dalai Lama: Spiritual Leader of Tibet by Anne-Marie Sullivan, Kindle edition (Mason Crest, 2014)

Modern Heroes: Dalai Lama by Gary Smailes (Waverley Books, 2009)

Audio book

Puffin Lives – Dalai Lama (Reado, 2015)

Places to visit

Tibetan Collection, National Museum of Scotland, Edinburgh

Tibetan Peace Garden, next to Imperial War Museum, London

INDEX